PENNEY, Sue

Sikhism

WORLD BELIEFS AND CULTURES
Sikhism

Revised and updated

Sue Penney

Heinemann LIBRARY

www.heinemann.co.uk/library
Visit our website to find out more information about Heinemann Library books.

To order:
☎ Phone 44 (0) 1865 888066
🖹 Send a fax to 44 (0) 1865 314091
💻 Visit the Heinemann Bookshop at www.heinemann.co.uk/library to browse our catalogue and order online.

First published in Great Britain by Heinemann Library, Halley Court, Jordan Hill, Oxford OX2 8EJ, part of Harcourt Education. Heinemann is a registered trademark of Harcourt Education Ltd.

Editorial: Nancy Dickmann
Design: Steve Mead and Debbie Oatley
Picture research: Melissa Allison
Production: Alison Parsons

Originated by Modern Age Repro
Printed and bound in China by Leo Paper Group

13 digit ISBN: 978 0 431 11031 8

12 11 10 09 08
10 9 8 7 6 5 4 3 2 1

British Library Cataloguing in Publication Data
Penney, Sue
Sikhism. – (World Beliefs and Cultures)
1. Sikhism – Juvenile literature
I. Title
294.5
A full catalogue record for this book is available from the British Library.

Acknowledgements
The publishers would like to thank the following for permission to reproduce copyright material: p. 20 'A letter from the Guru' is from *The Sikh Symbols*, the Sikh Missionary Society (UK), 1985.

The publishers would like to thank the following for permission to reproduce photographs: Ann and Bury Peerless pp. **11, 21, 27, 28, 33**; Art Directors/Helene Rogers pp. **20, 40**; Circa Photo Library pp. **9, 10, 32, 35, 42**; Harjinder Sing Sagoo pp. **8, 14, 15, 19, 22, 24, 25, 26, 29, 31, 34, 36, 38, 39, 41, 43**; Hutchison p. **37**; Impact p. **30**; Phil and Val Emmett pp. **6, 12, 17, 18, 23**; Topfoto p. **4**; World Religions Photo Library pp. **13** (P.Gapper), **16** (Christine Osborne). Background image on cover and inside book from istockphoto.com/Bart Broek.

Cover photo of the Golden Temple at Amritsar reproduced with permission of Getty Images/ National Geographic.

Our thanks to Philip Emmett for his comments in the preparation of this book.

Every effort has been made to contact copyright holders of any material reproduced in this book. Any omissions will be rectified in subsequent printings if notice is given to the publishers.

Contents

Any words shown in bold, **like this**, are explained in the glossary.

Dates: In this book, dates are followed by the letters BCE (Before the Common Era) or CE (Common Era). This is instead of using BC (Before Christ) and AD (*Anno Domini* meaning in the year of our Lord). The date numbers are the same in both systems.

Introducing Sikhism

Sikhs meet for worship in a building called a gurdwara.

Sikhs are followers of the religion called Sikhism. Sikhism began in the fifteenth century in the part of India called the **Punjab**. Today there are Sikhs in many countries of the world. The word Sikh comes from the **Punjabi** language, which was spoken by many of the first Sikhs. It means 'someone who learns' – in other words, a pupil or follower.

Gurus

Sikhs follow the teachings of **Gurus**. In India, the word guru is a title which is often given to respected religious teachers. Sikhs believe that there were ten Gurus who came to the world to give God's teachings to human beings. These are the teachings which Sikhs believe show them how to live. The first Guru of the Sikhs was a man called Guru Nanak. He chose his successor who, in turn, chose his successor, and so on. The tenth Guru said that after him there would be no more living Gurus. Instead, the Sikhs' teacher would be their holy book. This is why the

Sikhism fact check

- Sikhism began in India in the fifteenth century.
- It was begun by Guru Nanak. Guru means 'respected teacher'.
- Sikhs believe that Guru Nanak was the first of ten Gurus who were particularly important.
- The Sikh holy book is now their Guru and is called the Guru Granth Sahib.
- The Sikh place of worship is called a **gurdwara** or 'Guru's door'.
- Sikhs often call God **Satnam** which means 'True name' and **Raheguru** (often spelled **Waheguru**), which means 'wonderful Lord'.
- There are about 24 million Sikhs in the world today, most of whom live in the Punjab and neighbouring Indian states. More than 1 million live in other parts of the world – about 500,000 in the UK, 400,000 in Canada, 350,000 in the US and the rest in small communities in Europe, East Asia, Africa and Australia.

Sikhs' holy book is called the **Guru Granth Sahib**. The word Guru can also mean 'God', Granth means 'book' or 'collection' and Sahib is a title which shows respect. One way of translating this name is therefore 'the collection of the teachings of God'. The Guru Granth Sahib is always treated with great respect, because Sikhs believe it is the word of God, and the way in which they can learn about God. It plays an important part in all Sikh worship.

What do Sikhs believe?

Sikhs believe that there is one God who is almighty and **eternal** (existing for ever). Sikhs believe that God made the universe and everything in it, and is present everywhere and in everything. Human beings cannot comprehend God, but God is good and cares about everything in creation. One of Guru Nanak's **hymns** says, 'You are our mother and father and we are your children.' God is a spirit who should be loved, prayed to and worshipped. Sikhism teaches that God is the greatest Guru and it is wrong to worship anything except God.

Sikhs believe that God created male and female, but is a formless spirit who is neither male nor female. Guru Nanak said, 'God is neither a woman nor a man nor a bird.' Sikhs therefore take care not to describe God as being male or female, which is why they never use 'he' or 'she' when referring to God.

Guru Nanak taught that all human beings are equal, and are equally loved by God. This means that everyone should be treated in the same way, regardless of who their parents were, what job they do – or do not do – and whether they are a man or a woman. The way a person lives and his or her actions make that person good or evil.

Sikhs do not believe that theirs is the only religion which is right. They believe that all religions are different paths to finding God. This means that they respect other people's beliefs, and do not try to dissuade other people from practising their religion. They welcome people who decide for themselves that they want to join the Sikh faith.

The Sikh symbol

The symbol for Sikhism is made up of two swords, a symbol of fighting for what is right. Between them is a circle, a symbol that God is one, and without beginning or end. In the centre is a two-edged sword called a **khanda**, which gives its name to the symbol.

The Sikh symbol is called a khanda and is a symbol of the power of God.

The Sikh Gurus

The first Guru of Sikhism was called Nanak. He was born in 1469 CE in a village in northern India called Talwindi. Today the town is called Nankana Sahib, in honour of the Guru, and is in Pakistan. Nanak's parents were **Hindus**, and they wished Nanak to follow the traditions of Hinduism, too. When he grew up, he began work in a government office. Today, we would describe him as an accountant. The people who worked in the office were **Muslims**, and their beliefs were very different from the beliefs of Hindus. Nanak was a very religious young man and enjoyed talking to people about their beliefs. He learned a lot about the two religions. Nanak married when he was nineteen, and he and his wife had two sons.

A traditional picture of Guru Nanak.

Nanak's vision

One morning when he was about 30 years old, Nanak went to bathe in the river as usual. Then he disappeared. People searched for him for three days but they could find no trace of him. Everyone thought that he must have drowned. Then he returned, but he did not speak for a whole day. The first thing he said was, 'There is neither Hindu nor Muslim, only God's path. I shall follow God's path.' Nanak told the people that whilst he was away he had been taken to see God, and had been blessed. He had had a **vision** in which he had been shown that it is not the religion that people follow which is important; it is the way people live which really matters, and this comes from knowing God. Nanak said that he had been told by God to spend the rest of his life teaching people. In India, a respected teacher of religion is called a guru, so from this time on, Nanak was known as Guru Nanak. He called himself Nanak Das, which means 'Nanak the servant of God'.

For the next 20 years, Guru Nanak travelled. He made four long journeys, going to Varanasi, the holy city of Hindus, and to many other places in India. He went to Arabia and the Muslim holy city of Makkah, and the countries that today are called Iraq, Tibet and Sri Lanka. Wherever he went, Guru Nanak taught people. His message was that the way to find God was in the way you live and what you believe, not by following the outward practices of a religion without being sincere.

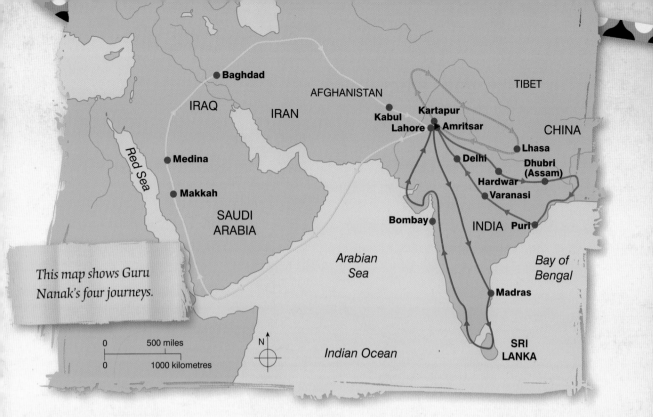

This map shows Guru Nanak's four journeys.

The first Sikhs

At last, Guru Nanak settled in a village called Kartapur in northern India. A group of people who wanted to follow his teachings came to live nearby. They became the first Sikhs, people who came to learn from the Guru. They met together to **meditate** in the morning and evening, to listen to Guru Nanak preach, and to join in singing the hymns which he composed. The followers often ate together, and this became an important part of their life in Kartapur. Free food was given to everyone, no matter what religion or social group they came from. In India at that time there were very strict divisions between different groups of people, and it was unheard of for people from different groups to eat like this. Guru Nanak said that it was very important.

One man who came to join the group was called Lehna. He became one of Guru Nanak's closest followers. Just before he passed away (Sikhs avoid saying that Gurus died), in 1539, Guru Nanak chose Lehna to be the next Guru. He gave him a new name, Angad, which means 'part of me'. Guru Angad was to carry on the work which Guru Nanak had begun.

Choosing the new Guru

There is a story about how Guru Nanak chose Lehna to succeed him. The story says that Guru Nanak set a test to see who would be the best person to be Guru. Guru Nanak dropped a cup into a muddy ditch and asked his two sons to get it for him. Both sons refused, because they felt it was beneath their dignity as the Guru's son to do a servant's job. Angad jumped down into the ditch and fetched the cup without even being asked. Guru Nanak obviously felt that this showed that Angad had a sense of service and humility which his own sons did not possess.

The other nine Gurus

Following Guru Nanak there were nine other Gurus. Each one was chosen by the one before, and continued Guru Nanak's teaching. Sikhs believe that all the Gurus shared Guru Nanak's spirit. They say that the Gurus were like lamps lit from each other. The ten Gurus all worked in different ways to develop the new faith. Guru Nanak once said, 'The Guru is the Ladder; the Guru is the Boat; the Guru is the Raft to take me to the Lord's name.'

Guru Angad (1539–52 CE)

Guru Angad was chosen by Guru Nanak, because he was so devoted and humble. He provided education for young people, and encouraged the Sikhs to study, to make sure that Sikhism continued. Guru Nanak spoke Punjabi, but at that time it did not have an accurate written form. Guru Angad made a collection of Guru Nanak's hymns, and felt that it was important for them to be written down. He developed the **Gurmukhi** alphabet in which the Sikh Scriptures are written. Gurmukhi means 'from the mouth of the Guru'. Guru Angad wrote some hymns himself that carry on the teachings of Guru Nanak. He also began the building of gurdwaras where Sikhs could worship. He instructed one of his followers, a distant relative called Amar Das, to begin a new Sikh town at Goindwal, near what is now Amritsar, in the Punjab.

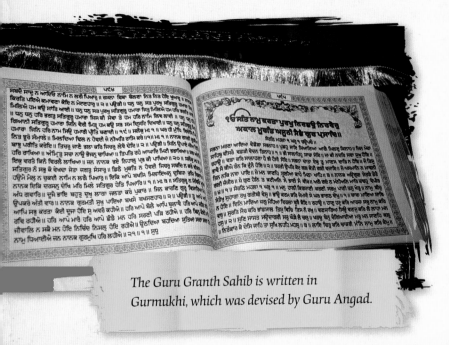

The Guru Granth Sahib is written in Gurmukhi, which was devised by Guru Angad.

One day a Hindu came to see Guru Angad, and happened to arrive when he was eating. Many Hindus are vegetarian, and the Hindu was uncomfortable at seeing the Guru tucking into a meal which included meat. Guru Angad said, 'The meats that should be avoided are envy, greed, selfishness, telling lies about other people and taking over other people's rights. There is life in everything, but what is eaten while remembering God is like nectar itself.' Before he died, aged 48, Guru Angad appointed Amar Das to be the next Guru.

Guru Amar Das (1552–74 CE)

You can find the places mentioned in this book on the map on page 44.

Guru Amar Das was 73 when he became Guru. He began a planned expansion of Sikhism, including beginning to build a new city at Amritsar to be its holiest place. He chose 94 men and 52 women to go out and preach to people about the new faith. Giving women an equal role with men was very unusual in those days. Guru Amar Das began the custom of Sikhs meeting at Goindwal, where he lived, three times a year at festival times so that they could listen to the Guru's teaching. This meant that he could meet them all in person. It helped to give the new religion its own identity. Guru Amar Das also continued Guru Nanak's teaching about the importance of eating together. Everyone who came to see him ate the **langar**, the meal which everyone shared. Once, Emperor Akbar came to see him, and the Guru insisted that he too should sit and eat with everyone else. The tradition of serving langar continues in all gurdwaras today. It is so important that it has also given its name to the room where it is eaten. Before he died aged 95, Guru Amar Das appointed his son-in-law Jetha as the next Guru.

Guru Ram Das (1574–81 CE)

Jetha took the name Guru Ram Das, which means 'servant of God'. He continued building the Sikh city of Amritsar, which had been begun on the instructions of Guru Amar Das. He encouraged tradesmen to settle there, and it became a great trading and religious centre. Guru Ram Das encouraged Sikhs to work together and help others. He is remembered especially for writing the **Lavan**, the wedding hymn which is used at all Sikh weddings.

> ## What a Sikh should be like
>
> *He who calls himself a Sikh of the True Guru, he must get up in the morning and say his prayers. He must rise in the early hours and bathe in the holy tank. He must meditate on God as advised by the Guru, and rid himself of the afflictions of sins and evil. As the day dawns he should recite scriptures, and repeat God's name in every activity.*
> (Guru Amar Das)

Everyone who attends worship in the gurdwara can share the langar, the meal which ends Sikh worship.

Guru Arjan (1581–1606)

Guru Arjan was the first Guru who was born a Sikh. He was the youngest son of Guru Ram Das. He continued the building at Amritsar begun by his father, and built a beautiful gurdwara, in the middle of an artificial lake there. This gurdwara is the **Harimandir Sahib**, often called the Golden Temple, the holiest building in the world for Sikhs. Guru Arjan collected together the writings of the first four Gurus, some of his own writings and some writings from Hindu and Muslim holy men. He organized them together into a book, called the **Adi Granth**. It was installed in the Golden Temple with great ceremony in August 1604 CE. Guru Arjan instructed everyone to bow to it, saying that it was a book of divine inspiration – in other words, its contents were inspired by God.

The tree at the Golden Temple, Amritsar, under which Baba Buddha sat.

Baba Buddha (1506–1631), a great Sikh

Baba Buddha is remembered as one of the greatest Sikhs. He knew the first six Gurus. He was a boy herding cattle when Guru Nanak visited his village. He served the Guru milk, and Guru Nanak exclaimed that though he was only a boy, he was a Buddha (old man) in his understanding. Baba Buddha became a highly respected Sikh and was responsible for the ceremony in which the five Gurus after Guru Nanak were installed as Guru. Baba Buddha supervised the building of the Golden Temple, and was appointed the first **granthi** (person who reads from and looks after the Guru Granth Sahib) there in 1604. The tree under which he sat to watch the building work still exists today. Near it is a shrine to his memory. He died at the age of 125 in 1631. His funeral was performed by Guru Har Gobind.

Guru Har Gobind (1606–44)

Guru Har Gobind became Guru when his father Guru Arjan was killed (see page 32). Guru Har Gobind realized that the Sikhs needed to form an army so that they could defend themselves with force if they had to. As a sign of this, the Guru always wore two swords. One showed his willingness to fight if necessary, the other was a sign of spiritual power. He was Guru for nearly 40 years, and he worked hard to make sure that many Sikhs became excellent fighters. When he died in 1644, he chose his grandson to become the next Guru.

Guru Har Rai (1644–61)

Guru Har Rai worked to make Sikhism stronger. During the time he was Guru, Sikhism spread more widely in northern India. He tried to make peace in the wars between the Sikhs and Muslims, and organized the opening of hospitals and dispensaries to treat people who were poor. Before he passed away, Guru Har Rai chose his son to be the next Guru.

The Gurdwara Bangla Sahib in New Delhi commemorates the life of Guru Har Krishan.

Guru Har Krishan (1661–64)

Guru Har Krishan was only five when he became Guru. He is mainly remembered for the way he cared for people. He died when he was only eight. He was helping to care for people who had smallpox when he caught the disease himself.

Guru Tegh Bahadur (1664–75)

Guru Tegh Bahadur was the son of Guru Har Gobind. Guru Tegh Bahadur was beheaded by the Emperor Aurangzeb in 1675, because he refused to change his religion (see page 33.) Sikhs remember Guru Tegh Bahadur with pride because he was ready to give up his life, but not his faith.

Guru Gobind Singh (1675–1708)

Guru Gobind Singh became the tenth Guru when he was only nine years old. He is remembered as being the most important Guru after Guru Nanak. He began the **Khalsa**, the fellowship of Sikhs who are full members of the religion. All the other Gurus had chosen a new Guru before they passed away, but Guru Gobind Singh said there would be no more living Gurus. The holy book contained the Gurus' teachings, and in future it would be the Sikhs' only teacher. Since that time, it has been called the **Guru Granth Sahib**.

These men are dressed to commemorate the panj piare – the beloved ones – who were willing to die for their beliefs.

The Khalsa

During the time of the tenth Guru, Guru Gobind Singh, Sikhs were being persecuted and killed for what they believed. The Guru decided that they needed to form an organized fighting force which could defend the faith.

In 1699, crowds of Sikhs gathered at Anandpur, in northern India, for the spring festival of Baisakhi. When the Guru spoke to them, he praised them for their loyalty and told them they needed to be strong to fight the people who were persecuting them. He drew his sword and asked if any Sikhs were willing to die for what they believed. No one answered. The Guru repeated the question. Still no one answered. The Guru asked a third time, and one man stepped forward. The Guru took him into his tent. There was a thud, and the Guru returned with a blood-stained sword. The Guru asked the question again. Another man came forward, saying he was prepared to die, too. The same thing happened. Three more men were taken away, one by one. The people were terrified, thinking that the Guru had killed all five men.

Jarnail's view

Jarnail Singh Grewal is 15, and lives in Nairobi, Kenya.

I love hearing the story of the beginning of the Khalsa and the panj piare. It makes me feel really proud that there were men who believed so strongly that they were ready to face death like that. I know lots of Sikhs and members of other religions have died in battle, but I think the panj piare were even braver, because it was a cold, conscious decision to step forward. I wonder what I would have done if I'd been there! I think listening to stories like this helps us to understand our history. It also helps us when we look at our own lives – Sikhs in Africa haven't had an easy time during the last hundred years, and it's important to remember that it's not just us, we are part of a long tradition. What we do might change the lives of Sikhs in the future.

You can find the places mentioned in this book on the map on page 44.

The beginning of the Khalsa

After the fifth time, the Guru went away. When he returned soon afterwards, all five men were with him! They were dressed in saffron-yellow robes, just like his own. Guru Gobind Singh explained that this had been a test of courage and loyalty to the Guru. The community had passed the test. The Guru told the people that because the men had been prepared to die for what they believed, they should be called the **panj piare** – the beloved ones. They would be the first members of a new group. It would be called the Khalsa, which means 'the pure ones'. Sikhs could only belong to this group if they were without fear, and ready to die for their faith. When the people understood what the Guru wanted, many more men and women came forward to become members of the Khalsa.

Amrit

The Guru said that being part of the Khalsa was more important than anything else, so to show that they were all equal they should do two things. One was to drink **amrit** from the same bowl. Amrit is a special mixture of sugar and water which is stirred with a khanda, the two-edged sword. The importance of drinking it from the same bowl was that in those days, people from different backgrounds never ate or drank together. Drinking from the same bowl was even more unheard of than eating with others, as Sikhs had done since the time of Guru Nanak. After he had given the five men amrit, Guru Gobind Singh asked them to give it to him. Sikhs say that this shows his humility – he became a follower at the same time as he became a leader.

The Sikh family

The second thing to show their equality was to use the same name. This was a symbol that they were all one family. Men were to take the name Singh, which means 'lion'. Women were to take the name Kaur, which means 'princess'. Since that time, all Sikhs have used these names as part of their own name. The Guru also told them that from that day on, they were to wear five symbols of their faith. These are the symbols which Sikhs still wear today, which are called the **five Ks** (see page 20).

Drinking amrit (a special mixture of sugar and water) is still an important part of Sikh worship today.

The history of Sikhism

For the first 200 years of the new religion, Sikhs were led by ten Gurus. During this time, Sikhism developed and began to find its identity. Important changes were made by the tenth Guru, Guru Gobind Singh. In 1699, he began the Khalsa, the fellowship of Sikhs. This was the event which really made Sikhism a separate religion.

One reason why the Khalsa was necessary was that Sikhs were being persecuted for their beliefs. India had been part of the Moghul Empire for 200 years, and at first the emperors had allowed religious freedom. Later Muslim emperors like Jehangir (1605–27) and Aurangzeb (1658–1707) tried to impose their own religion, and Hindus and Sikhs were persecuted and killed for refusing to give up their faith. After Guru Gobind Singh's death, groups of Sikhs joined together to fight for their faith and for their own country. From 1708 to 1739 was the worst period of persecution in Sikh history. Anyone known to be a Sikh was in danger of being killed. Gurdwaras, the Sikh places of worship, either closed or were cared for by Hindus, and many Sikhs began following their religion in secret and did not wear the five Ks or a **turban**.

Ranjit Singh was a Sikh emperor for 40 years.

Ranjit Singh

From 1739, as the Moghul Empire broke up, foreign armies began to invade India. Sikhs fought and won battles on the edges of the Punjab, and gradually, independent Sikh states were established. The ruler of one of these states was a young soldier called Ranjit Singh (1780–1839). He won control of the other Sikh states, and eventually declared himself the ruler of an empire which included the whole of the Punjab and much of northern India. He ruled for 40 years, and many Sikhs think of this as being a 'golden age' for Sikhs. Sikhs had freedom from persecution, and Ranjit Singh was a good ruler. However, little was done to promote the teachings of the Gurus.

After Ranjit Singh

After the death of Ranjit Singh the Sikh empire collapsed, and in 1849 the British took control of the Punjab as they increased their rule over India. The British respected Sikhs for their bravery, but did little to preserve Sikhism as a separate religion. Sikhs struggled to maintain their identity, and it was only in 1909 that Sikhs in India won the right to hold their own marriage services rather than have weddings conducted by Hindu priests. After years of peaceful protests, Sikhs were eventually granted the right to manage their own gurdwaras in 1925.

The gurdwara at Makindu in Kenya.

After Partition

When India became independent in 1947, the new country of Pakistan was created. The border between what was then West Pakistan and India cut through the middle of the Punjab. Many Sikhs were bitterly disappointed. They had hoped that Sikhs would be given their own country. Sikhs felt they had to leave Pakistan, and thousands of people were killed in riots. Sikhs in India felt that they were treated unfairly, and their leaders began a protest campaign. After years of unrest, things came to a head in 1984, when fighting between Sikhs and Hindus led to the Indian government taking direct control. The then Prime Minister, Indira Gandhi, ordered the Indian army to occupy the Punjab and to attack the Golden Temple in Amritsar, where Sikhs whom they described as terrorists were hiding. Thousands of Sikhs were killed, and the holiest places of Sikhism were badly damaged. The attack caused much anger and bitterness among Sikhs all over the world. Since then, there have been difficulties in relations between the Indian government and Sikhs. Some Sikhs would still like more autonomy for the Punjab and other provinces of India.

Sikhs in other countries

During the days of the British Empire, skilled workers including Sikhs were taken from India to Africa to help build roads and railways. Many Sikhs settled in East Africa, and became established and successful there. After the countries became independent, many were ruled by military dictators, and some became jealous of the Indians' success. For example, in 1972 Idi Amin, the tyrannical President of Uganda, forced all Indians in the country to leave. During the 1970s, many Sikhs left Africa and moved to the UK, Canada and the US. During the early 1990s, a new Ugandan government returned all confiscated property to Indians who had been expelled, and invited them back. Punjabi is now an official language in several East African countries.

The Guru Granth Sahib

In a gurdwara, the Guru Granth Sahib is kept on a special throne called a takht.

The most important of the Sikh holy books is the Guru Granth Sahib. It was begun by the first Guru, Guru Nanak. He composed hundreds of hymns praising God, and 974 of them are in the Guru Granth Sahib. In 1604 CE the fifth Guru, Guru Arjan, had an official collection of hymns put together. This contained the hymns of Guru Nanak and hymns written by the other Gurus. It also contained hymns written by Hindu and Muslim holy men whose teachings are in agreement with the teachings of the Gurus. It is very unusual for the holy book of one religion to contain writings by members of other religions. The hymns praise God, and say what God is like. They also include advice about the right way to live. This book is called the Adi Granth. Adi means 'first' (that is, most important), Granth means a 'book' or 'collection'. The Harimandir Sahib was built especially to house this book. The Adi Granth still exists today, and Sikhism is the only major religion in the world which still has the first copy of its holy book.

How the Guru Granth Sahib was completed

In 1706 CE, the tenth Guru added to the Adi Granth hymns which had been written by his father, the ninth Guru, and said that this made it complete. Before he died, Guru Gobind Singh said that the book should be the next and only Guru, and it was therefore called the Guru Granth Sahib. Since that date, nothing has been added or taken away from it. For nearly 200 years, copies of it were written out by hand, very carefully so that no mistakes were made. The first copy was printed in 1852, after much discussion. The ruling council of Sikhs decided that every copy should be exactly the same, and so today every copy of the Guru Granth Sahib has the same number of pages – 1430 – and particular hymns are always to be found on the same page. Translations into other languages including English exist, to help understanding, but they are never used in place of the original version.

The language of the Guru Granth Sahib

When Guru Amar Das was gathering together the writings of the Gurus to form the Adi Granth, he used Gurmukhi, the language in which Punjabi is written. Punjabi was the language which the people spoke. Hindu holy books were written in Sanskrit, a language only used in worship. The Guru was asked why he had not used Sanskrit, as might have been expected for holy books in India. The Guru replied, 'Sanskrit is like a well, deep, inaccessible and confined to the elite. The language of the people is like rainwater, ever fresh, abundant and accessible to all.' This shows how he wanted the holy books to be used.

Gutkas

Some Sikhs have their own copy of the Guru Granth Sahib at home. They believe that because it is so important, it should not be placed on a shelf like other books. It should have a room of its own, as a human Guru would. This room then becomes a gurdwara, because the Guru Granth Sahib is there. For many Sikhs, of course, this is not possible. Instead, most have a smaller book called a **gutka**. This contains the most important hymns and the daily prayers. Like the Guru Granth Sahib, a gutka is treated with great respect, and is wrapped in a cloth when not being read. Before reading from it, a Sikh washes his or her hands.

Other holy books

No other holy book is as important for Sikhs as the Guru Granth Sahib. However, there are other books which contain important Sikh writings. The Dasam Granth ('Book of the tenth Guru') contains hymns which were written by Guru Gobind Singh and 52 other poets who worked for him. Some of these poems are used in Sikh worship. The Hukamnamas are letters written by the Gurus to their followers. There are also books which help to explain parts of the Guru Granth Sahib. These are used when the hymns are being explained as part of the service in a gurdwara. Sikhs use the Rahit Maryada as a guide to how they should live. This was put together by the Sikh ruling council in the Punjab, the Shiromani Gurdwara Parbandhak Committee, in 1945.

This Sikh is reading a gutka, which contains important hymns and prayers.

What the Guru Granth Sahib says

Sikhs believe that the Guru Granth Sahib contains God's truth, as it was shown to the Gurus. This is the reason why they treat it with such great respect. The Guru Granth Sahib is used in all Sikh worship, and wherever there is a Guru Granth Sahib it automatically becomes a gurdwara. It takes the most important place in the gurdwara. Weddings are held in front of it, and it is used to help in the naming of babies. An important part of worship is taking guidance from the Guru Granth Sahib. This is done by opening the book at random and reading the first line of the first complete hymn on the left-hand page. This is called 'taking the **vak**'. The vak is usually written out and placed on a notice board at the gurdwara entrance so that everyone attending the gurdwara during the day may benefit from it.

When the Guru Granth Sahib is being carried, it is always held above the person's head as a sign of respect.

Respect for the Guru Granth Sahib

During the day, the Guru Granth Sahib is kept on a stool called a **manji**, resting on a cloth and three cushions, with a canopy over it. While it is open, there is generally someone sitting behind it. It is not usually left unattended. The person sitting in attendance holds a **chauri**, a fan made of hair or feathers. This is a symbol of authority, and is waved over the Guru Granth Sahib periodically, in the same way as it would have been waved over the head of a king or prince in India. When it is closed, a Guru Granth Sahib is carefully covered with special cloths called **rumalas**. There is a special ceremony at night called **Sukhasan** when the Guru Granth Sahib is 'put to bed'. The reverse ceremony in a morning is called **Parkash karna**. Carrying the Guru Granth Sahib is a great honour. It is always held above the person's head.

The words of the Guru Granth Sahib

The whole of the Guru Granth Sahib is written in poetry, arranged in stanzas (groups of lines) called **shabads**. The opening words of the Guru Granth Sahib are Guru Nanak's description of what God is. This shabad is called the **Mool Mantar**, and is often said to sum up Sikh beliefs about God.

The Mool Mantar

There is one and only one God
Whose name is Truth.
God the creator is without fear, without hate,
immortal,
Without form, and is beyond birth and death,
And is understood through the Guru's grace.

This is how Guru Nanak describes the call from God to preach:

I was a minstrel, out of work, when the Lord
took me into His service.
To sing His Praises day and night,
He gave me His Order, right from the start.
My Lord and Master has summoned me,
His minstrel, to the True Mansion of His
Presence.
He has dressed me in the robes of His True Praise and Glory.

The Ambrosial Nectar of the True Name has become my food.
Those who follow the Guru's Teachings,
who eat this food and are satisfied, find peace.
His minstrel spreads His Glory,
singing and vibrating the Word of His Shabad.
O Nanak, praising the True Lord, I have obtained His Perfection.
(Guru Granth Sahib, page 150)

The letters in the centre of this wall-painting mean 'There is only one God.'

At the time of Guru Nanak, women were often treated as second-class citizens. Sikhism has always taught that men and women are to be treated equally. This passage shows why Guru Nanak believed this was important.

From woman, man is born;
within woman, man is conceived;
to woman he is engaged and married.
Woman becomes his friend;
through woman, the future generations come
So why call her bad? From her, kings are born.
From woman, woman is born; without woman, there would be no one at all.
(Guru Granth Sahib, page 473)

The five Ks

Everyone who is a full member of the Sikh religion must wear five symbols which show that they are Sikhs. Many other Sikhs choose to wear them, too. They are usually known as the five Ks, because in Punjabi, the language which many Sikhs speak, their names all begin with the letter K. The five Ks were introduced by the tenth Guru, Guru Gobind Singh, as part of the ceremony in which he began the Khalsa. Each of them reminds Sikhs of something about their religion, and they are worn by both men and women.

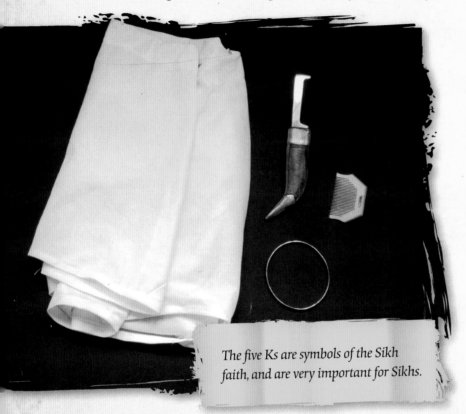

The five Ks are symbols of the Sikh faith, and are very important for Sikhs.

Kesh

Kesh means 'uncut hair'. Guru Gobind Singh said that hair should be allowed to grow naturally. For men, this includes not shaving. At the time of the Guru, some holy men let their hair become tangled and dirty. This was supposed to show how holy they were, because they were not thinking about their body. The Guru said that this was not right. Hair should be allowed to grow, but it should be kept clean and should be combed at least twice a day.

A letter from the Guru

Soon after the ceremony in which he told Sikhs to wear the five Ks, in June 1699, Guru Gobind Singh wrote a letter to Sikhs living in Kabul, in what is today called Afghanistan. This is part of what he said:

I am much pleased with you all. You must take the baptism of the sword from five; keep your hair uncut – this is the seal of the Guru. Never be complacent about the pair of shorts and the sword. Always wear on your wrist a steel bracelet, keep your hair neat and clean and comb it twice a day. Always read and recite the hymns of the Guru. Meditate on the name of the wonderful Lord – God alone. Keep the symbols of the faith as the Guru has told you.

Kangha

The **kangha** is a small wooden comb. It keeps the hair fixed in place, and is a symbol of cleanliness. For Sikhs, keeping clean and tidy is part of their religion. Combing their hair reminds them that their lives should be tidy and organized, too.

Kirpan

The **kirpan** is a short sword. It reminds Sikhs that it is their duty to fight against evil. A kirpan should never be used for attack, only for defence. It may be up to a metre long, but most Sikhs today carry one which is about 10 cm (4 inches) long. It is usually kept in a special wooden case, fixed to a strap over the person's shoulder.

This Sikh boy is tying his turban.

Kara

The **kara** is a plain steel bangle worn on the right wrist. It is worn as a symbol, not as jewellery. It is a complete circle, which reminds Sikhs that there is one God and one truth, without beginning or end. The steel reminds them of the strength they must have when fighting for what is right.

Kachera

Kachera are short trousers, worn as underwear. At the time of Guru Gobind Singh, when they were introduced, most people in India wore long, loose clothes. Guru Gobind Singh said that the change in style was a symbol that people were leaving behind old ideas and following better ones. Kachera were also more practical, especially in battle.

The turban

The turban is not one of the five Ks, but most male Sikhs and some female Sikhs wear one. A turban is a piece of cloth about 5 metres (16 feet) long, which is wound tightly around the head and tucked in to keep it in place. At the time of Guru Gobind Singh, many important people in India wore turbans as a sign of power. The Guru wore one as a sign of the power of the Sikhs. His followers copied him, and the custom continued. The turban has become an important symbol of the Sikh faith. Young boys may wear their hair tied in a **patka**, a small turban, before they are given their first proper turban at about the age of eleven. In Britain and some other countries, there have been problems over the wearing of turbans. Sikhs have faced prejudice and ignorance, and it has taken time for the rules governing uniforms which include caps or helmets to be changed so that Sikhs can wear turbans instead.

Sikh gurdwaras

The Sikh place of worship is called the gurdwara. This means 'Guru's door'. One of the meanings of the word Guru is 'God', so this is like saying that a gurdwara is God's house. A gurdwara does not have to be a special building – many of the first gurdwaras were tents. Gurdwaras may be specially built, they can also be in ordinary houses or other buildings. The important thing is not the building, it is the fact that the Guru Granth Sahib is there.

Ideally, a gurdwara should have separate rooms near the entrance where men and women can wash their hands and feet, but some are not large enough for this to be possible. At the Golden Temple, people enter by walking through running water. No one wears shoes in the worship room so there are always areas where people can leave their shoes. This is a large room where people meet for worship. If the building is large enough, there is also a small room where the Guru Granth Sahib is kept when it is not in the worship room. There is always a kitchen and dining room. It is part of Sikh worship that everyone present should be able to share a meal after the service. Larger gurdwaras may have a library, one or more classrooms and sometimes offices. Some gurdwaras have guest rooms where people can stay overnight. Sikhs are expected not to smoke or drink alcohol, so these things are not allowed in a gurdwara.

Sikhs meet for worship inside the diwan hall of a gurdwara.

The worship room

The proper name for the worship room is the **diwan hall**. It is often decorated with tinsel and small lights. Sometimes there are pictures of Guru Nanak and the other Gurus on the walls. Some Sikhs do not approve of this because they think people may begin to worship the pictures, rather than God. A diwan hall usually has a carpet, but there are no seats. Everyone attending worship sits on the floor, as a sign that everyone is equal. The most important part of the room is the platform at one end. This is called the **takht**, which means 'throne'. The Guru Granth Sahib is placed upon it, on a special stool called a manji. The takht is the same sort of throne as a living guru would sit on, and shows that the book is treated with the same respect. In front of the takht is a place where people can place offerings of food or money.

The outside of a gurdwara (notice the Nishan Sahib, the Sikh flag, which always flies outside the gurdwara).

The langar

Sikh services are always followed by a meal called the langar. Everyone who has attended the service is welcome at the langar, too. It is an important part of Sikh worship which goes back to the days of Guru Nanak and is a symbol of the Sikh belief that all people are equal. Food is cooked and served by both men and women, and given free to everyone. It is paid for by donations which people give at the beginning of services, and by other offerings. The meal is simple and wholesome, and no matter where in the world the gurdwara is, the langar always consists of dishes which would be eaten in the Punjab. The food is vegetarian, so that people who do not usually eat meat can still take part.

Outside the gurdwara

Specially-built gurdwaras may have a dome and decorations on the outside, but these are not always used, and especially outside India many gurdwaras are in ordinary houses. Whatever the building is like, all gurdwaras have a yellow flag with the Sikh symbol on it outside. This is called the **Nishan Sahib**. It always flies above the level of the building.

The Sangat

The Sangat is the community of Sikhs who worship at a particular gurdwara. There is no idea in Sikhism of people cutting themselves off from others, or living apart. Everyone who attends the gurdwara regularly is an equal member of the Sangat. Gurdwaras also have committees, elected every year, which organize events and details about how the gurdwara is run. Sikhs believe that the community is very important, and especially outside India the gurdwara is a focus where people can meet and socialize as well as worship. Most gurdwaras run classes in Punjabi and music where young people can learn more about Sikhism, the Guru Granth Sahib and how it is used during worship.

Worship in the gurdwara

Sikhs do not have a particular day of worship. Outside India, the main services are usually held on a Sunday, because it is convenient for many people. Many gurdwaras are open from dawn to sunset every day, with services in the morning and evening. Many gurdwaras employ someone whose job is to read from the Guru Granth Sahib and to lead the prayers. This person is called the granthi. Any Sikh who is respected by the others may lead the worship in a gurdwara, and any Sikh who can read Gurmukhi may read the Guru Granth Sahib. The person reading sits behind the takht, facing the people.

Any Sikh who can read Gurmukhi can read the Guru Granth Sahib in the gurdwara.

The most important room in a gurdwara is the diwan hall or worship room where Sikhs meet together in the same place as the Guru Granth Sahib. Before going into the diwan hall, everyone takes off their shoes. They may wash their hands and feet, or have had a bath at home before coming to the gurdwara. Anyone who is not wearing a turban covers their head. These things show respect for the Guru Granth Sahib. When they go into the room, people go to the front and leave an offering of food or money in front of the takht where the Guru Granth Sahib is. They bow or kneel in front of it, often touching the ground with their forehead. As they go to sit down, people are careful never to turn their backs on the throne, which would show great disrespect. The people sit on the floor to show that everyone is equal, and that the Guru Granth Sahib is the most important thing in the room. It is usual for men and women to sit on opposite sides of the room.

Worship

Services in a gurdwara are usually held in Punjabi, the language spoken by most Sikhs. They may last up to five hours, but they are very relaxed, and people are not necessarily expected to stay for the whole time. Even though people may move around, the atmosphere is quiet and respectful.

The aim of Sikh worship is to give praise to God. Most worship consists of reading and singing of shabads (hymns) from the Guru Granth Sahib, and from other books like the writings of the Gurus. The singing is called **kirtan** and is very important. It is done by musicians called **ragis**, who usually play tabla (drums) and harmoniums.

24

The people do not usually join in the singing. A service may include a talk, which helps to explain the shabads, or is about things which affect Sikhs in their lives.

The Ardas

All services end with the **Ardas**, a special prayer which lasts about eight minutes. Everyone stands with hands folded, facing the Guru Granth Sahib. One person leads the prayer, standing in front of the rest. The first part reminds everyone to remember God and the ten Gurus, and to pass on the teachings of the Guru Granth Sahib. Then prayers are said for Sikhs and all people everywhere. There may be special prayers for people who are ill or who need special prayers for some other reason.

Whilst the Ardas is being said, the **karah parshad** is stirred with a kirpan. Karah parshad means 'holy sweet'. It is a special 'pudding' made of equal quantities of flour or semolina, sugar, water and ghee (specially prepared butter). It is mixed in an iron bowl and given to everyone who has attended the service, as a symbol that everyone is equal. At the end of the service, everyone shares the langar.

Shinder's view

Shinder is 16. She is an orphan, and lives with her cousins in Doncaster, UK.
I came to England when my mother died five years ago. At first, everything felt very strange, and it took me a long time to get used to a different way of life – especially the cold! It was then that I really started to enjoy going to the gurdwara. I'd never really thought about it much at home – it was just something we did. Here, it helped to make me feel at home, because so much of it was familiar. My favourite part of the service is the part of the Ardas when we pray for all Sikhs everywhere. I think about all my friends here and friends I had in the Punjab.

Sikh worship is led by musicians called ragis.

You can find the places mentioned in this book on the map on page 44.

The Harimandir Sahib, Amritsar

Sikhs believe that every gurdwara is equally important, because each one contains the Guru Granth Sahib. However, the Harimandir Sahib at Amritsar is a very special gurdwara. Harimandir Sahib means 'Temple of God'. It was begun when Guru Amar Das, the third Guru, asked Ram Das (later the fourth Guru) to build a place which would be a central meeting point for Sikhs. Work began on excavating the lake in 1577, and was finally completed by the fifth Guru in 1588. Then work began on the Temple, which was completed in 1601.

The Temple stands in the middle of the lake called the Pool of Nectar. It is reached by a causeway 60 metres (197 feet) long. The platform on which it is built is 20 metres (66 feet) square. The Temple itself is 12 metres (39 feet) square, surrounded by a marble walkway. Many Sikhs wanted this building to be high and splendid, but Guru Arjan reminded them of Guru Nanak's teaching about humility, and it was built to the lowest elevation possible. It has entrances on all four sides, to show that Sikhism is open to all. Guru Arjan said, 'My faith is for the people of all castes and all creeds from whichever direction they come and to whichever direction they bow.'

The Golden Temple in Amritsar is the most important shrine for Sikhs.

The Golden Temple

The Temple has been damaged several times during its history. In 1764 it was rebuilt in marble and the Sikh ruler Ranjit Singh ordered the upper half of the building to be covered in copper sheets overlaid with gold. Since then it has been known as the Golden Temple. The walkway which surrounds the lake is called the **parkama**, and is made of marble. Each side is about 150 metres (492 feet) long. On the side away from the water are shrines to famous Sikhs, and memorials to Sikhs who have died in battle.

Sikhs walk around it in a clockwise direction, and may scatter rose petals or lay garlands at the shrines.

The walls of the Golden Temple have verses from the Guru Granth Sahib carved on them, and inside there are very old hand-written copies of the Guru Granth Sahib. They are not opened, but other copies around the Temple complex are read, and can be heard around the area. Readings and singing of shabads (hymns) begin at dawn, and go on until late at night every day.

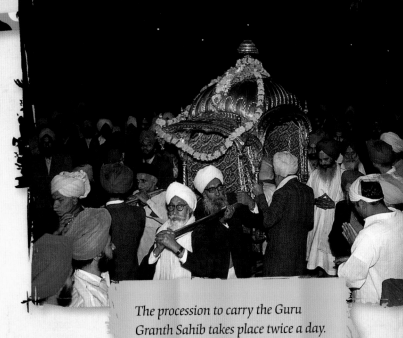

The procession to carry the Guru Granth Sahib takes place twice a day.

Carrying the Guru Granth Sahib

There is a special procession at five o'clock every morning and at ten o'clock every night when the Guru Granth Sahib is carried to and from the worship room to the room where it spends the night. This room is in a building called the Akal Takht, opposite the Harimandir Sahib. The Guru Granth Sahib is carried, resting on cushions and pillows, on a **palki**, which is a palanquin (rather like a covered stretcher). It is wrapped in silk and muslin, and showered with rose petals. It is carried to and from the palki by the Head Granthi, who rests it on a special cushion on his head. To take part in the procession to carry the palki to or from the Harimandir Sahib is a great honour for Sikhs, and the short journey may take up to half an hour while hundreds of worshippers take part in it.

While the Guru Granth Sahib is being read during the day, thousands of worshippers pass through the Temple. There is a special kitchen where karah parshad is prepared, and worshippers may make a donation and take some of this to the attendants at the doors of the Harimandir Sahib. The attendants then give it to people leaving. Sikhs believe that this is a way of passing on God's blessings. There is also a langar where thousands of people eat each day.

What Guru Nanak said

This quote from the Guru Granth Sahib shows why Guru Nanak taught his followers not to go on pilgrimages:

If a man goes to bathe at a place of pilgrimage, and he has the mind of a crook and the body of a thief, of course his outside will be washed by the bathing, but his inside will be twice as unclean. He will be like a gourd which is clean on the outside but full of poison on the inside. The saints are pure without such bathing. The thief remains a thief even if he bathes at places of pilgrimage. (Guru Granth Sahib, page 789)

The five Takhts

Of the thousands of gurdwaras in the world, five are considered to be the most special. They are called the Five Takhts (thrones), and are all connected in different ways with the first Gurus.

Akal Takht

Akal Takht means 'eternal throne'. The Akal Takht is at the other end of the causeway which leads to the Harimandir Sahib, the Golden Temple in Amritsar. Its foundation stone was laid by Guru Har Gobind, and he was installed as Guru there in 1606. It is the place where the Guru Granth Sahib is kept at night, after it has been in the Harimandir Sahib during the day. Sikhs say that this is symbolic. The Harimandir Sahib is a symbol of spiritual guidance; the Akal Takht is a symbol of justice and the social life of the Sikh community. For hundreds of years, it was the place where the Sikh ruling council met. However, during the attack by the Indian army in 1984, the Akal Takht was badly damaged, and rebuilding it has taken many years.

The Akal Takht in Amritsar was rebuilt after it was almost destroyed in 1984.

You can find the places mentioned in this book on the map on page 44.

Celebrations at Takht Keshgarh Sahib

In April 1999, the Takht Keshgarh Sahib and the town of Anandpur were the scene of a huge gathering of Sikhs from all over the world. They were celebrating the 300th anniversary of the establishment of the Khalsa by Guru Gobind Singh, which took place on 14 April 1699. Anandpur's usual population is about 15,000, and the number of people visiting for this festival has been estimated at about 1.5 million! The main entrances into the town were decorated with white painted gateways, and buildings in the town were painted white, too. Part of the celebrations included processions of Sikhs who had marched from each of the places where the first five beloved ones (panj piare) were born. The streets were filled with Sikhs of all shapes, sizes and nationalities, specially decorated trucks and buses, horses and their riders, and elephants. There were displays of horsemanship and other martial arts, as well as specially arranged worship in the gurdwaras of the town and in special tents set up to cope with the crowds of people. Sikhs who were present said it was an occasion they would never forget.

Takht Damdama Sahib

This gurdwara is in the town of Talwindi Sabo, near Bhatinda in the south of the Punjab. It is the place where Guru Gobind Singh lived for nearly a year in 1706, putting together the final edition of the Guru Granth Sahib. This edition was carried into battle by Sikh troops, but was lost during a battle in 1721. However, the text was preserved because a number of copies had been made of it, so it is still the official version from which all other Guru Granth Sahibs are taken.

Takht Keshgarh Sahib

This gurdwara is in the town of Anandpur, in a valley near the Himalaya mountains. It is built on the site where the head of Guru Tegh Bahadur was cremated after he had been beheaded. Anandpur is also the place where the tenth Guru began the Khalsa. Some of the Guru's weapons are kept in a museum next to the gurdwara, including the actual khanda (two-edged sword) with which he stirred the amrit in the first Khalsa ceremony.

Takht Keshgarh Sahib in Anandpur is built on the site where Guru Tegh Bahadur's head was cremated.

Takht Hazur Sahib

Hazur Sahib is a gurdwara on the banks of the river near Hyderabad in Maharashtra. It marks the place where Guru Gobind Singh died, and the central room is built over the spot where his body was cremated (incinerated). There is a museum in the gurdwara where some of the Guru's clothes are kept. There is also a horse which is descended from one belonging to the Guru, which is used in gurpurb processions in the town.

Takht Patna Sahib

This gurdwara is in the town of Patna, the capital of the state of Bihar. It is the place where Guru Gobind Singh was born. Patna was also visited by Guru Nanak and Guru Tegh Bahadur.

Celebrations

The Sikh calendar is called the Nanakshahi calendar, and years are counted from the birth of Guru Nanak in 1469. 2005 CE is therefore 536 Nanakshahi, 2010 CE is 541 Nanakshahi etc. In 1999 CE, changes were made to this calendar which means that it follows a solar year rather than a lunar year as it did before. This means that dates according to the Western Common Era calendar will not change from year to year as they used to. New Year is Chet 1 which in the Common Era calendar is 14 March.

Handing out sweets is part of the celebrations for Baisakhi at a gurdwara in London.

Baisakhi

Baisakhi is the spring festival and it is celebrated by Sikhs all over the world. In the Western calendar, Baisakhi falls on 14 April. The first Baisakhi took place in 1567 CE. In 1699 CE, Guru Gobind Singh began the Khalsa, the Sikh fellowship, during Baisakhi. This is why it is now often a popular time for holding the amrit ceremony, the special ceremony for people who wish to become full members of the Sikh religion.

At Baisakhi, there are celebrations at the gurdwara all day. The service begins soon after dawn, and lasts for hours, with people arriving and leaving, staying for as long as they can. The langar, the meal which is part of Sikh worship, is often served all day. There are readings from the Guru Granth Sahib, and poems which remind people of the first Baisakhi and how important the day is. Like many other Sikh festivals, there are processions which include the Guru Granth Sahib being carried on a float – a lorry or other open vehicle – followed by people singing religious songs. In many places in India there are fairs to celebrate Baisakhi. In the town of Amritsar, a famous market is held every year, where farmers buy and sell all kinds of animals.

Changing the Nishan Sahib

Part of the celebrations for Baisakhi is renewing the Nishan Sahib. This is the saffron-yellow flag, showing the Sikh symbol, which flies outside every gurdwara. The colour symbolizes the fact that Sikhs are ready to give up their lives for God. During the day of the Baisakhi festival, a service is held outside the gurdwara, led by five men representing the panj piare, the first members of the Khalsa. The flagpole is taken down, and the chola, the yellow cloth which covers the pole and the flag, is removed. The flagpole and the flag are washed. The chola is always replaced, and a new flag may be used, too. Then the flag is re-hoisted. This is often a big community event. After the flag has been successfully re-hoisted, everyone stands for the Ardas prayer, the prayer which ends all Sikh services.

As well as the amrit ceremony, at most gurdwaras the festival of Baisakhi is celebrated in other ways. There are often competitions which cover many subjects – music, poetry, sports, essay-writing and public speaking, as well as Sikh history. The competitions are a way of encouraging Sikhs, especially young people, to celebrate the festival and to remember its importance.

Replacing the covers on the Nishan Sahib, the flag which flies outside every gurdwara.

Akhand Path

An **Akhand Path** is a continuous reading of the Guru Granth Sahib from beginning to end without stopping. It forms an important part of most Sikh festivals. An Akhand Path takes about 48 hours, and is usually timed so that it ends early in the morning. When the reading is part of a festival, it is arranged so as to end on the morning of the celebrations. The reading is done by any members of the local Sikh community who can read Gurmukhi clearly and accurately. They take it in turns, reading for no more than two hours at a time. There is always a 'reserve' in case someone is ill. The readers make sure that no break occurs, with a new reader taking position behind the Guru Granth Sahib as the previous reader comes to the end of their section. The readers have a bath before going to the gurdwara, and immediately before beginning to read they wash their hands, so that they are clean to touch the pages of the Guru Granth Sahib. Whilst an Akhand Path is taking place, Sikhs make a special effort to go to the gurdwara, to listen and meditate. They try very hard to be there for the special ceremony which ends the reading. Langar is served throughout the Akhand Path, so a rota of volunteers is also needed to cook, serve and wash up.

Gurpurbs

A gurpurb is a Sikh festival which celebrates the birth or death of one of the Gurus. The name means 'a holy day in honour of the Guru'. Sikhs do not attach a lot of importance to the actual date of festivals, and especially in Western countries the celebrations are often held the following weekend.

The birthday of Guru Nanak

Sikhs all over the world celebrate Guru Nanak's birthday in November. The celebrations usually last for three days. In towns or cities where there are large numbers of Sikhs, there are processions through the streets. The people in the procession sing hymns written by Guru Nanak. People watching are often offered sweets or fruit and non-alcoholic drinks as a reminder of Guru Nanak's teaching about how important it is to share food.

The birthday of Guru Gobind Singh

Guru Gobind Singh was the tenth Guru, and he was born in 1666 CE. His birthday is celebrated in December, with processions. One of the most important is in the town of Patna in north-eastern India, where the Guru was born. There are also games and sports competitions to celebrate the festival. In many gurdwaras, songs written by the Guru are sung as part of the celebrations.

The Guru Granth Sahib is carried on a decorated float during the gurpurb processions.

The death of Guru Arjan

Guru Arjan was the fifth Guru. Sikhs think of him as the first Sikh **martyr**. A martyr is someone who dies for his or her beliefs. Guru Arjan refused to give up his Sikh faith, even though the ruler of the country had ordered that he must. The ruler ordered that Guru Arjan should be killed, and he was tortured to death by having hot sand poured over his body.

Like other gurpurbs, Guru Arjan's death is remembered with processions. He was killed in the summer, when it is very hot in India, and his thirst was part of his torture. To remind people of his suffering, and as a sign of respect, people watching the processions – whatever their race or beliefs – are offered cold, non-alcoholic drinks.

The death of Guru Tegh Bahadur

Guru Tegh Bahadur was the ninth Guru. Sikhs are particularly proud of him because he gave his life on behalf of Hindus. At that time the Islamic rulers of that part of India were persecuting Sikhs and Hindus. Hindu leaders came to Guru Tegh Bahadur, asking for help, because he was a holy man. The Guru told the Hindus to tell the Emperor that Hindus would accept Islam if Guru Tegh Bahadur could be persuaded to accept it. As a result, the Guru was arrested and taken to the Moghul Emperor.

Guru Tegh Bahadur was offered many rewards if he would change his religion, but he would not accept any of them. Then the Guru was made to watch whilst three of his followers were tortured to death. Even this did not make him change his mind. He still said that anyone who worshipped God should be allowed to worship as they wished.

This gurdwara at Delhi is built at the place where Tegh Bahadur was killed.

The rulers realized that they would not succeed in making the Guru change his mind, and ordered that he should be beheaded. He died for his belief in freedom of worship. Sikhs say that to die for your own religion is very brave, but Guru Tegh Bahadur was even braver, because he died to save someone else's religion.

The main gurpurb to remember Guru Tegh Bahadur's death is held in Delhi, the capital of India, where he was killed. The processions lead through the streets to a beautiful gurdwara, built on the site where he was beheaded, where the people go to worship.

Processions

The processions which are part of a gurpurb are called nagar kirtan, and are an important part of the celebrations. The processions are always organized in the same way. They are led by five people representing the panj piare, the five men who were the first to join the Khalsa. They wear yellow robes, usually with a wide blue belt, and yellow turbans. Behind them is a beautifully decorated float carrying the Guru Granth Sahib, resting on cushions and carefully looked after. Behind this come all the people, singing shabads and other religious songs. In Delhi, the capital of India, about 22 km (10 miles) of roads are decorated for the procession celebrating Guru Nanak's birthday. The procession itself may be up to 7 km (about 3 miles) long.

At Divali, the Golden Temple and its precincts are surrounded by coloured lights, and there are firework displays.

Melas

Sikhs celebrate two main sorts of festival. The more important ones are gurpurbs, which celebrate the birth or death of a Guru. Other festivals are **melas**, which means 'fairs'. Melas are often similar to Hindu festivals, but Sikhs celebrate them in their own way. Many melas take place in particular towns or areas, and celebrate events which were particularly connected with that place.

Like all Sikh festivals, melas are celebrated as opportunities to care for other people. Sikhs often give money to charity, and offer their time and talents in looking after others. This is part of **sewa**, the teaching about the importance of caring for others which is an important part of Sikh belief. In India and in the United States, for example, Sikh doctors and dentists may offer free treatment to anyone who needs it as a way of celebrating the festival, and many Sikhs give food to the poor.

Divali

Divali means 'festival of lights'. It takes place on 7 November. Its name comes from small clay lamps called divas. The Sikh celebrations of the festival were begun by Guru Amar Das. At Divali, Sikhs remember when Guru Har Gobind was released from prison, in 1612. He returned home to Amritsar, and the people were so delighted that they lit lamps in every house to welcome him home. To celebrate the story, and to remind people of it, Sikhs today illuminate the whole of the area around the Harimandir Sahib in Amritsar with hundreds of coloured light bulbs, and there are wonderful firework displays. Fireworks, bonfires and lighting candles are part of the Sikh celebrations for Divali all over the world.

The release of Guru Har Gobind

This is the story about Guru Har Gobind which Sikhs remember at Divali.

Guru Har Gobind was the sixth Guru. He had been imprisoned by the Emperor, who was called Jehangir. The Guru was accused of raising an army against the Emperor, and of committing treason against him. When the charges were investigated, they were found to be totally false. The Emperor said that the Guru could be released, and he was told he could leave just before the festival of Divali in 1619. However, while he had been in the prison, Guru Har Gobind had met 52 Hindu princes (rajas) who had also been falsely accused and imprisoned. Guru Har Gobind refused to leave the prison unless the 52 rajas were released with him. Jehangir thought that he would get the better of the Guru, so he said that he could take with him as many of the rajas as could hold on to his cloak. The condition was that they all had to leave by a particular gateway. This was very narrow, and only one man could squeeze through at a time. The Guru arranged for 52 long tassels to be stitched onto his cloak, so that all the rajas could hold it. Everyone was freed.

Hola Mohalla

The festival called Hola Mohalla is celebrated in the town of Anandpur in India. It is held on 17 March, and every year it is attended by thousands of people. It was started by Guru Gobind Singh in 1680 CE. He organized military exercises and mock battles for the Sikhs who had gathered there. It was arranged for the day following the Hindu festival of Holi. This was important because it was a way of helping to establish Sikh identity. Today, the mock battles and displays of swordsmanship and horse-riding still continue. There are also sports events and music and poetry competitions, which are all ways of reminding

Sword fights and displays are part of Hola Mohalla.

Sikhs of the festival which the Guru began. There are also meetings for worship and the singing of hymns from the Guru Granth Sahib. The festival ends with a large procession, which is led by people carrying the Nishan Sahibs (Sikh flags) from all the gurdwaras in the area.

Family occasions

Birth

As soon as possible after a baby is born, someone present repeats the Mool Mantar. This means the first thing a baby hears are the most important Sikh beliefs. Parents may share their joy at the birth by giving sweets or other small presents to friends and neighbours. It is the custom for relations to visit soon after the birth, and give presents for the baby.

The naming ceremony

The naming ceremony is called **nam karan**. It is part of a normal service at the gurdwara. It usually takes place within a few weeks of the baby's birth, although it can be later. The baby's parents and other relations go to the gurdwara, to thank God for the new baby, and to choose its name. (Babies usually have a pet name which is used before the official name is given.) It is the custom for parents to give a new rumala (the cloth used for covering the Guru Granth Sahib when it is not being read) and to pay for the karah parshad which everyone shares at the end of the service.

When a baby is being welcomed, the Ardas prayer at the end of the service includes the names of the parents, and thanks God for the gift of the baby. At the end of the prayer, the parents go to the front of the gurdwara, and lay the baby on the floor in front of the Guru Granth Sahib. The granthi opens the Guru Granth Sahib at random (that is, without choosing a particular page). He or she reads the first new verse on the left-hand page, then tells the parents which letter of the alphabet began the first word of the verse.

Giving the baby a drop of amrit is sometimes part of the naming ceremony.

The parents then choose a name that begins with this letter. When the parents have chosen the name, the granthi announces it to the congregation, and says, 'Jo bole so nihal' (this is a way of showing approval that does not really translate into English). The congregation shouts, 'Sat siri akal' (God is truth) to show their agreement. Then everyone shares the karah parshad and congratulates the new parents.

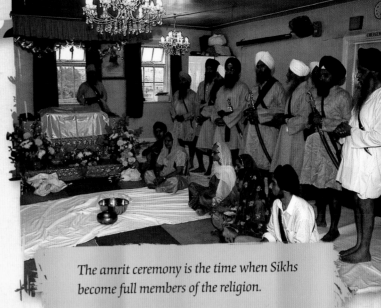

The amrit ceremony is the time when Sikhs become full members of the religion.

The amrit ceremony

The amrit ceremony is the ceremony in which people become members of the Khalsa. It is expected that only people who are mature enough to understand the commitment will take part in this ceremony, so those taking amrit are at least in their teens. Many Sikhs delay it until middle age, and some never take it.

The amrit ceremony must take place in front of the Guru Granth Sahib, but in private. Therefore it cannot take place in the worship room, which is open to anyone. Apart from those who wish to join, only six Sikhs are present. They must all be **amritdhari** (members of the Khalsa) themselves. Five Sikhs represent the panj piare, a sixth reads from the Guru Granth Sahib. The people who wish to join are required to wash their hair, cover their heads and wear clean clothes and the five Ks.

Sikh names

Sikhs use the same names for both males and females. Often, the only way of telling by their name whether a Sikh is male or female is because males also have the name Singh, females also have the name Kaur. Many Sikh men use Singh as their surname, and many women use Kaur. Others may use it as a middle name, and their family name as their surname. Traditionally, a Sikh woman does not take her father's name or her husband's name, but in Western countries, Mr Singh's wife may find she is called Mrs Singh, because many non-Sikhs do not know how Sikh names are given.

The ceremony

The basic beliefs of Sikhism are explained, and one of the five amritdhari repeats the duties which members of the Khalsa must keep. Those taking amrit agree to accept these duties. There are prayers and readings from the Guru Granth Sahib. Those joining kneel on their right knee with the left knee raised. This is a symbol that they are ready to rise to defend their faith. Each person drinks some of the amrit, and it is sprinkled onto their eyes, hair and hands. After more prayers, the ceremony ends with everyone eating karah parshad. After they have taken part in this ceremony, Sikhs are expected to keep all the rules and duties of their religion.

Marriage

The Sikh marriage service is called **anand karaj** which means 'ceremony of happiness'. The Gurus taught that family life was very important, and being married is part of this. Many Sikh weddings are arranged marriages, and even if the couple have suggested their marriage the families are very involved. The bride must be at least eighteen, and a marriage cannot take place unless both bride and groom agree to it.

A bridegroom is prepared for the marriage ceremony.

Sikh weddings usually take place in the morning. They must always take place in front of the Guru Granth Sahib. In India, they are often held in the open air. In other countries, they are usually held in the gurdwara. The ceremony may be performed by the granthi, but any Sikh may officiate, provided that he or she has been chosen by both families.

On the evening before the wedding, the bride's friends and female relatives have a party at her house. She is given money and special sweet foods, and they paint beautiful patterns on her hands and feet with a henna dye which lasts for several days.

On the morning of the wedding, the bridegroom and his relatives go to the bride's house, and are given refreshments. Presents such as lengths of cloth for turbans or clothing are exchanged. Then everyone goes to the gurdwara, or wherever the marriage is to take place. The bridegroom usually wears a red or pink turban and has a scarf around his neck. He sits at the front, in front of the Guru Granth Sahib. The bride's father puts a garland of flowers on the Guru Granth Sahib. The bride enters, with her sister or other female relative. She wears red, often with beautiful gold jewellery. After bowing to the Guru Granth Sahib, she sits down next to the bridegroom. Her father gives her a garland of flowers.

The couple and their parents stand while the **Ardas** prayer is said. This is a way of asking God's blessing on the marriage. The person leading the ceremony gives a talk about marriage and what it means for Sikhs. The couple are asked if they understand and accept their responsibilities to each other as husband and wife. They show that they agree to the marriage by bowing in front of the Guru Granth Sahib. The bride's father places one end of the bridegroom's scarf in his hand and the other end in the bride's hand. This is a symbol that they are being joined together as husband and wife. They hold on to it for the rest of the ceremony.

The bride and groom are joined with a scarf, a symbol that they are being joined together as husband and wife.

The most important part of the ceremony is the reading of the Lavan, a hymn written for weddings by Guru Ram Das. It has four verses, each explaining something about marriage. They are spoken one at a time, and then sung. During the singing, bride and groom walk in a clockwise direction around the Guru Granth Sahib. When they have done this for the fourth time, they are married. Everyone stands to join in the Ardas prayer, and there may be speeches before everyone shares the karah parshad. A meal follows, which may be held in the langar room.

Divorce

Traditionally, divorce was very rare within the Sikh community. Among Sikhs who live in Western countries it is now a little more common, though still far more rare than in society at large. If the marriage cannot be saved, divorce is allowed, and either person may marry again in the gurdwara.

Jo-Ann's view

Jo-Ann is 16, and lives in Ontario, Canada. Last fall, my friend Surjit asked if I would like to go to her sister Rani's wedding. I'd never been to a Sikh wedding, and it was real interesting. Surjit explained what would happen and what some of the symbols were, and I was glad about that, because I didn't understand the Punjabi at all. Some parts of the service were in English, though. Rani was so beautiful with all her jewellery on, but she was very nervous. Her new husband Jarwal looked very proud. The only bit I didn't enjoy was the karah parshad at the end. Surjit had told me that this was a sacred food and it would be very rude to refuse it, but I didn't like the taste at all. The wedding was great – it was a day I'll remember for ever.

Death

Sikhism teaches that the body is only the outer shell, and what matters is the person's **soul**. This is the spirit which they believe moves on from one body to another after death. This belief is called **reincarnation**. Guru Nanak said that reincarnation explains why life so often seems to be unfair, because the things you have done in a past life can follow you, and affect your present life. This is called your **karma**. Your karma decides the circumstances into which you will be born. By living a good life and helping others you can become closer to God, and with God's help you can become good enough to break out of the rebirth cycle. Then you will not be reborn, but will live with God for ever.

Sikhs say that death is like going to sleep. Just as you go to sleep when you are tired, and wake up ready for another day, so at the end of life you die and are reborn. Death is the end of one life, but the beginning of another one. They say that it is natural for people who are left to feel sorrow, but they should also remember that the person who has died has gone on to another life. The Guru Granth Sahib says, 'The dawn of a new day is the message of a sunset.' Death is part of life and God's will, so displays of grief such as wailing or crying loudly are discouraged.

At a Sikh funeral, prayers are recited before the body is burned.

Sikh funerals

After a person has died, their body is washed by relatives of the same sex, and dressed in the five Ks. Then it is wrapped in a white sheet. If the person has not died at home, the body is brought there for relatives and friends to come and pay their last respects. A Sikh who has died is usually cremated, which means their body is burned. If this is not possible, burial on land or at sea is permitted. In India, cremation usually takes place on the day of death, because India is a hot country. The body is taken in procession or a motorcade either to a **funeral pyre** on the bank of a river or, in cities, to a crematorium. In Western countries, the funeral takes place as soon as possible after death, and the body is taken to a **crematorium**. It is usual for male relatives to help to place the body in the incinerator, in the same way that traditionally in India they would help to lift it on to the funeral pyre.

In Western countries, male relatives help to carry the coffin at the crematorium.

At the crematorium the Ardas prayer is recited, asking for peace for the person's soul and the **Kirtan Sohila** is said. This is the prayer said by every Sikh before they go to sleep at night, and so helps to remind people that death is like sleep. After the body has been burned, the ashes and the kirpan and kara which, being metal, will not burn are usually scattered on running water. This may be the sea or a river. Sikhs living in other countries sometimes have the ashes flown back to the **Punjab** so that they can be scattered there.

When someone dies, there is usually a reading of the Guru Granth Sahib at the person's home or the gurdwara. It is usually read in sections in the morning and evening, and is called a **Sadharan Path**. It is not an Akhand Path because it is not a non-stop reading. It is timed to last ten days, which is the time of the official period of mourning. Sikhs believe that reading the Guru Granth Sahib like this gives comfort to the relatives of someone who has died.

Sikhs do not normally put up headstones or other memorials to people who have died. They believe people should be remembered for the good things they did during their life, rather than their memory being focused on a memorial stone. Stones are also forbidden to make sure that the memorial does not become a place for worship.

A hymn by Guru Tegh Bahadur

This verse is read at Sikh funerals:
Why believe that the mortal body is permanent? It passes away like a dream in the night, like the shadow of the clouds. Those who realize that the world is unreal seek protection in God.

What it means to be a Sikh

Meditation is an important part of life for many Sikhs.

As individuals

Sikhism teaches that God is in the soul of every person, in the same way that the properties of a whole ocean are present in a single drop of water. Therefore individuals should look after the body which houses the soul. Sikhism discourages fasting or other practices which may harm the body. Healthy eating, doing good actions and thinking good thoughts are part of looking after the body. So is doing a worthwhile job, and doing it to the best of your ability. Guru Nanak once said, 'Do your daily duties with hands and feet but concentrate on the Lord.'

Sikhs try to follow the teachings of the Gurus and the teachings of the Guru Granth Sahib in their daily life. The duties of a member of the Khalsa are to recite the five sacred prayers every day, and to give up all ideas of caste and class differences. There are also four actions which are forbidden. These are to cut hair, to use harmful (non-medicinal) drugs like alcohol or tobacco, to commit adultery (have a sexual relationship with someone to whom you are not married), and to eat meat which has been killed according to Muslim or **Jewish** practice (where the animal has been killed by cutting its throat). Many Sikhs who are not members of the Khalsa choose to adopt these restrictions in their own life, too.

All Sikhs are expected to get up early and have a bath before meditating on the name of God. There are specific prayers for morning and evening, which Sikhs know off by heart. They may recite the **japji sahib**, the morning prayer, as they are getting ready for work. As well as the set prayers, Sikhs may also pray at any other time they wish.

The rich man and the poor man

A popular Sikh story sums up how important way of life is for Sikhs. It says that on one of his journeys Guru Nanak visited the village of Saidpur in West Punjab. He stayed with a poor man called Lalo. A rich man, Bhago, in the same village, was very offended that the Guru had not chosen to stay with him. The story says that Guru Nanak took two pieces of bread, one from Lalo's house and one from Bhago's. As he squeezed them, milk dripped from Lalo's bread, but blood came from Bhago's. Guru Nanak said that this was because Lalo was honest, even though he was poor, but Bhago had made his money by taking advantage of others. Bhago promised to live a better life in the future. The Guru Granth Sahib says, 'There is no worship without good deeds.'

In the community

Sikhs believe that everything was created by God, and therefore all human beings have a spark of God in them. This is what lies behind the Sikh teaching about sewa – service to others. This is a fundamental part of Sikhism, and means that all Sikhs should try to do what they can to serve others – not just other Sikhs, but anyone in the community in which they live. Service may involve giving money – Guru Gobind Singh said that if they could, Sikhs should give a tenth of their income to help others. Sikhs accept that for some people this is not possible. Also, if someone is rich, giving money may be very easy. It may challenge them a lot more to give some time instead. Sewa often involves menial jobs – ones which people do not like doing. It may also involve cooking and serving the langar at the gurdwara, or looking after people who are poor or ill. In areas where many people are very poor, gurdwaras offer free food and medical treatment. In the West, many Sikhs work as doctors and nurses.

An important part of sewa is talking to people about God. This does not mean trying to persuade people to become Sikhs. Sikhism teaches that each person should follow the religion that is right for them. For much of his life, Guru Nanak spent time talking to Hindus and Muslims. He did not try to convert them away from what they believed in. The Guru taught that the way they lived was the most important thing, rather than just following the outward rituals of any religion without really thinking about it.

All Sikhs should do what they can to help others – jobs like cleaning the gurdwara may be part of this service.

Map

The globe on the right shows the location of the map below.

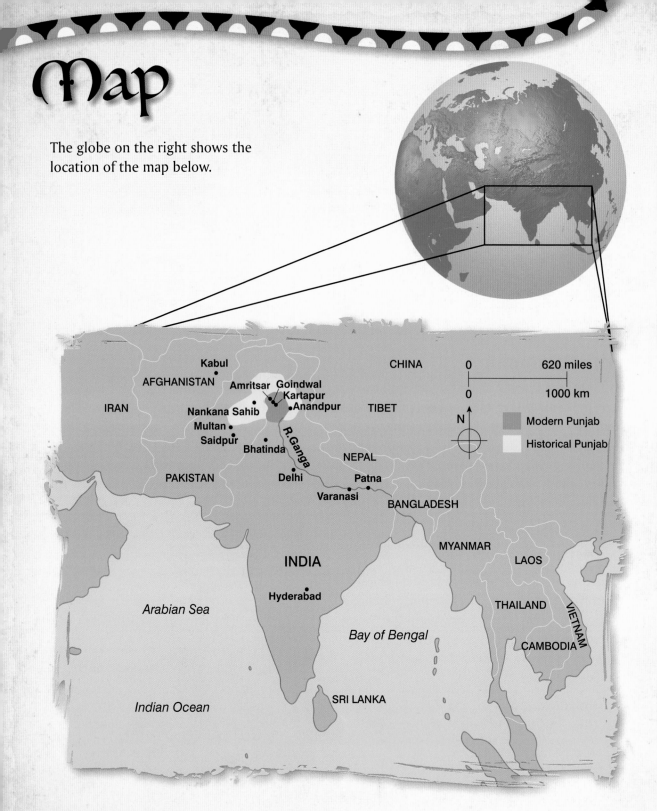

Place names

Some places on this map, or mentioned in the book, are called by different names today:

Myanmar – Burma

Nankana Sahib – Talwindi

River Ganga – River Ganges

Sri Lanka – Ceylon

Varanasi – Benares.

Timeline

Major events in world history

BCE	3000–1700	Indus valley civilization flourished
	2500	Pyramids in Egypt built
	1800	Stonehenge completed
	1220	Rameses II builds the Temple of Amon (Egypt)
	1000	Nubian Empire (countries around the Nile) begins and lasts until c350 CE
	776	First Olympic games
	450s	Greece is a centre of art and literature under Pericles
	336–323	Conquests of Alexander the Great
	300	Mayan civilization begins
	200	Great Wall of China begun
	48	Julius Caesar becomes Roman emperor
CE	79	Eruption of Vesuvius destroys Pompeii
	161–80	Golden Age of the Roman Empire under Marcus Aurelius
	330	Byzantine Empire begins
	868	First printed book (China)
	c1000	Leif Ericson may have discovered America
	1066	Battle of Hastings, Norman Conquest of Britain
	1300	Ottoman empire begins (lasts until 1922)
	1325	Aztec Empire begins (lasts until 1521)
	1400	Black Death kills one person in three throughout China, North Africa and Europe
	1452	Leonardo da Vinci born
	1492	Christopher Columbus sails to America
	1564	William Shakespeare born
	1620	Pilgrim Fathers arrive in what is now Massachusetts
	1648	Taj Mahal built
	1768–71	Captain Cook sails to Australia
	1776	American Declaration of Independence
	1859	Charles Darwin publishes Origin of Species
	1908	Henry Ford produces the first Model T Ford car
	1914–18	World War I
	1929	Wall Street Crash and the Great Depression
	1939–45	World War II
	1946	First computer invented
	1953	Chemical structure of DNA discovered
	1969	First moon landings
	1981	AIDS virus diagnosed
	1984	Scientists discover a hole in the ozone layer
	1989	Berlin Wall is torn down
	1991	Break-up of the former Soviet Union
	1994	Nelson Mandela becomes President of South Africa
	1997	An adult mammal, Dolly the Sheep, is cloned for the first time
	2000	Millennium celebrations take place all over the world

Major events in Sikh history

CE	1469	Guru Nanak born
	1499	Guru Nanak's vision
	1506–1631	Life of Baba Buddha
	1539	Guru Nanak passes away
	1539–52	Guru Angad
	1552–74	Guru Amar Das
	1574–81	Guru Ram Das
	1575	Beginning of the building of Amritsar
	1577–88	Building of Lake for Temple
	1581–1606	Guru Arjan (first Sikh martyr)
	1588–1601	Building of Temple
	1604	Adi Granth put together and installed in the Harimandir Sahib
	1606–44	Guru Har Gobind
	1612	Release of Guru Har Gobind
	1644–61	Guru Har Rai
	1661–64	Guru Har Krishan
	1664–75	Guru Tegh Bahadur (died defending religious freedom)
	1675–1708	Guru Gobind Singh
	1699	Guru Gobind Singh establishes the Khalsa
	1706	Guru Granth Sahib completed
	1764	Temple rebuilt in marble and gold added to roof
	1780–1839	Ranjit Singh (great Sikh ruler)
	1864	First printed copies of Guru Granth Sahib made
	1909	Sikhs granted some autonomy of religion in India
	1925	Sikhs allowed to manage their own gurdwaras for the first time
	1945	Rahit Maryada put together by Sikh ruling council in Punjab
	1947	Creation of Pakistan splits the Punjab
	1984	Indian army attacks the Golden Temple
	1999	Tri-centenary celebration of the Khalsa
	2004	Fourth Centenary of the Adi Granth compilation
	2006	Fourth Centenary of Guru Arjan's martyrdom

Glossary

Adi Granth	Sikh holy book
Akhand Path	continuous reading of the Guru Granth Sahib, often as part of a festival
amrit	'nectar' – special mixture of sugar crystals and water
amritdhari	Sikhs who have taken amrit
anand karaj	'ceremony of happiness' – Sikh marriage
Ardas	formal prayer offered during most Sikh worship
arranged marriage	marriage where a possible partner is chosen or suggested by relatives
chauri	fan waved over the Guru Granth Sahib as a sign of respect
crematorium	place where dead bodies are incinerated
diwan hall	worship room in a gurdwara
eternal	lasting for ever, without beginning or end
five Ks	symbols of the Sikh religion worn by all Sikhs who have taken amrit
funeral pyre	special fire built to burn dead bodies
granthi	person who reads and looks after the Guru Granth Sahib
gurdwara	Sikh place of worship
Gurmukhi	written form of Punjabi
gurpurb	festival celebrating the birth or death of a Guru
Guru	respected teacher (for Sikhs, one of ten special teachers)
Guru Granth Sahib	holy book of the Sikhs
gutka	collection of Sikh hymns and prayers
Harimandir Sahib	'temple of God' – holiest shrine of the Sikhs in Amritsar, Punjab
Hindu	follower of the religion of Hinduism
hymn	religious poem, usually sung as part of worship
japji sahib	Sikh morning prayer
Jewish	following the religion of Judaism
kachera	shorts worn as underwear (one of the five Ks)
kangha	wooden comb (one of the five Ks)
kara	steel bangle (one of the five Ks)
karah parshad	'holy sweet' – sacred food shared at the end of Sikh worship
karma	actions from a previous life which affect this life
Khalsa	'Sikh fellowship' – established by Guru Gobind Singh in 1699, now a term used for full members of the religion
khanda	two-edged sword
kirpan	short sword (one of the five Ks)

kirtan	the singing of hymns in Sikh worship
Kirtan Sohila	Sikh night-time prayer
langar	meal served without charge as part of Sikh worship
Lavan	wedding hymn written by Guru Amar Das
manji	throne on which the Guru Granth Sahib rests
martyr	someone who dies for what they believe
meditate	training the mind to concentrate in a special way
mela	'fair' – Sikh festival
Mool Mantar	summary of Sikh teachings about God, and first words of the Guru Granth Sahib
Muslim	follower of the religion of Islam
nam karan	naming ceremony for a baby
Nishan Sahib	Sikh flag which flies outside all gurdwaras
palki	stretcher used for carrying the Guru Granth Sahib
panj piare	'beloved ones' – the first members of the Khalsa
parkama	walkway around the Golden Temple precincts
Parkash karna	ceremony in which the Guru Granth Sahib is made ready for reading in the morning
patka	small turban for young boys
Punjab	area of north-east India
Punjabi	Indian language spoken by most Sikhs
ragi	musician who leads the singing during Sikh worship
Raheguru (or Waheguru)	'wonderful Lord' – Sikh name for God
reincarnation	belief that a soul is reborn in another body
rumala	cloth used for covering the Guru Granth Sahib
Sadharan Path	non-continuous reading of the whole of the Guru Granth Sahib
Satnam	'true name' – Sikh name for God
sewa	service – caring for others
shabad	hymn from the Guru Granth Sahib
soul	person's spirit which lives on after death
Sukhasan	ceremony in which Guru Granth Sahib is 'put to bed'
takht	'throne' – used for the Guru Granth Sahib
turban	length of material wound around the head to cover it
vak	guidance from the Gurus obtained by opening the Guru Granth Sahib at random
vision	dream-like religious experience

Further Information

The Guru Granth Sahib and Sikhism, Anita Ganeri (Evans Brothers, 2002)
Guru Nanak and Sikhism, Rajinder Singh Panesar (Wayland, 2002)
India, Anita Roy (Raintree Publishers, 2006)
Sikhism, Geoff Teece (Franklin Watts, 2004)

Index